영역 시선집

맹숙영 시 / 원응순 역

바람 속의 하얀 그리움

The White Nostalgia on the Wind

도서출판 한글

Maeng Sook-Young's

The Korean-English Poetical Anthology

The White Nostalgia on the Wind

Trans. by Won Eung-Soon

HANGEUL PUBLISHING COMPANY

다시 오는 새벽

우주의 조그만 덩어리 하나
광속光速으로 다가온다
디지털 바퀴에서
별빛이 노랗게 눈을 뜬다
무수한 빛의 파장 일으키며
가슴에 와 안긴다
와락 끌어당겨 포옹하니
샘물 터져 흐르고
폭포수 내리는 물줄기에
수많은 별이 꽃으로 피어나
현란한 빛의 파노라마를 이루며
한 순간에 어둠을 덮어버린다
쏟아져 내리는 금빛 은빛 햇살
창을 투시하여 들어와
고요하고 평화로운 보금자리에
쌓이고 출렁인다

Prologue
Dawn Comes Again

One great mass in the universe,
Approaches here in the velocity of light.
And the star-light from the digital wheel
Opens its eyes in yellow color,
And throws itself in its bosom,
Making lots of wave lengths of light.
Pulling them with a jerk to embrace,
And spouting a spring out, with the
   waterfall's stream
Many stars come into bloom,
Forming a brilliant light's panorama
Covers darkness in an instant.
The pouring sunshines in silver or golden
   colors
Came in through the windows,
Fill and wave in a silent and peaceful nest.
This dawn

어제와는 다른 감동의 이 새벽
새로운 청사진을 펼치는
꿈을 먹고 시작하는
또 다른 파란 날이다

바람 속의 하얀 그리움

Of the deep emotion different with
  yesterday,
Is quite another blue day
Beginning with dream expanded by a new
  blueprint.

목　차

II. 드림 소나타 / *Dream Sonata*

III. 물음표 소고 / *A Little Thought on the Question Mark*

IV. 여행 스케치 / *Travelling Sketches*

V. 영혼의 메시지 / *A Soul's Message*

I.

봄 소나티나

Sonatina for Spring

꽃비는

익을 대로
무르익어
마침내 마다 않고
농익어버린
그대의 잔잔한 미소
향으로 흘러내린다

어디서 불어오는
바람 타고 살짝
사랑 젖어
흐른다

　　바람 속의 하얀 그리움

The Flowery Rain

Being fully ripened,
As far as it can mellow
At last freely
In your soft smile
Richly mellowed,
It overflows down as its aroma.

And it runs down
Soaked in love
Secretly on wind
Nowhere it blows.

초롱꽃

족두리 쓰고
꽃등 들고
멀리 발자국 소리
길 따라 불 밝힌다
곱게 단장한
고요로운 그 모습
앉은자리 꽃자리엔
임 기다리는
꽃 달만

A Bellflower

With its crown-like cap,
Getting a flowery lamp in hand,
Leaving footmark's sound faraway behind,
She brightens along the lane.
The silent figure,
Dressed beautifully
On her place where she sat,
Only a flowery moon
Is waiting her love.

꽃대궁

솟대 위에 앉은
봉황새
깃털 사이로
내려오는 햇살
한 줄기 끌어내려
대궁 속에 심고
해거름 녘
기다리는
개밥바라기

은빛 별 한 올
가닥 풀어
중심 잡고
볼을 간질이는
감미로운 바람도
한 자락
붙잡아 동여맨다

풀씨 하나 떠돌다
자리매김하러

The Floral Stalk

A phoenix,
Sat on the big stick,
Pulls down a ray of
The sunlight
Coming down between its feathers,
And planted in the floral stalk,
The Venus waits
For the sunset.

A thread of a silver star
Unloose a piece of it,
Keeping its balance,
And the soft wind
Tickling its cheeks
Ties up
A piece of it.

A seed of grass
Floating to take its place
In the peeping hour,

기웃거리는 시간
긴 터널 또 다른
우주를 향해
잉태를 꿈꿀 때
초록별들
반짝 눈을 뜬다

When it dreams pregnancy
Toward the different universe
Through the long tunnel,
The green stars
Open their twinkle eyes.

꽃을 피워낸 까닭은

누가 알까
맨살의 들판을
색색으로 물들여 놓은
저 꽃의 만발을
또 향기를
가슴 밑바닥에서
올라와 흘러넘치는
조각 난 상처를 달래는
눈물 강 때문일까
아픔이 쓰렸기에
고통 속으로 들어가는
영혼을 붙잡으려는
안타까운 발버둥이었을까
다시 태어나려는
한
줄
기
소망 때문일까

The Reason of Blooming Flowers?

Who knows?
The naked field,
The full blooms of that flowers
Dyed with various colors,
And with fragrance,
The reason is their tears,
Which soothe wounds into pieces,
And overflowing from the bottoms of their
 bosoms?
Or was that their anxious squirming,
That they would try to take the soul,
Going into pains by the hands?
Or is that
A
s
t
r
a
n
d
Of hope,
That is about to be born again?

봄을 엿보다

아홉 폭 치맛자락처럼
단정하고 의연한 자태
물빛 햇살 거느리고 오는
연분홍빛 그녀를 바라본다
멀리 능선 따라 강변 따라
언덕에도 수많은 꽃불 켜지고
꽃 향이 소용돌이친다
산마다 피어나는 꽃들의 미소
수줍음에 그녀의 얼굴이 붉다

바람 속의 하얀 그리움

Stealing A Glance at Spring

I look at her with soft pink color,
Coming near with water-colored sunlight
Having the figure
As decent and dauntless as her nine-folded
  skirt's tail
Lots of the flowery lights
Bloom along the far ridge-line
And along the riverside,
The flower's aroma swirls.
Her bashful face is red with the smile of the
  flowers
Blooming at every mountain.

덩굴장미

고 새빨갛게
입술 칠하고
고개 바짝 쳐들고
잰걸음으로
올라가더니 어디
그뿐이던가
앙큼하다 싶더니
맹랑하다

향기로 몰아붙이더니
아! 마침내
놀랍다, 가시
가시까지
지니고 있을 줄이야

바람 속의 하얀 그리움

A Wild Vine Rose

You,
With your lips plastered red,
And raising your head,
Climbing at the quick steps,
In addition to those,
You are not only over-ambitious,
But also unreliable.

Cornering us by your fragrance,
Ah, lastly
It's surprising
To have a thorn
Even a thorn.

나무도 봄앓이 하다

꽃샘 매운바람에도
의지의 다리로 서 있던 그
먼 산에서 손 흔들며 내려오는
꽃등불에 눈이 시다
몰려오는 꽃 향에
마른 가슴에도 촛불 켜지고
묵은 나이테로
가슴 겹겹이 싸매고
흐트러지지 않고 왔는데
웬일인가 감추어진
열일곱의 순정이 얼굴 붉힌다
열아홉 꿈 꿈틀대며 날개 펼친다
아니라 해도 꽃바람에 흔들리며
열꽃의 붉은 꽃망울로
부끄러움에 몸살 앓는다

The Tree Gets Spring Fever Too

The flowery light, coming down
Waving its hands from the far mountain
That it has stood as the leg of will against
  the spring cold,
Is dazzling to our eyes.
A candle light in the dry heart
Is lit by the driven aroma of flowers,
And its chest is tied up
By its old annual ring,
It came here without dispersing.
Then for some reason or other,
The secret pure heart of seventeen years
Reddens its face.
Nineteen years' dream spreads its wings,
Giving a wiggle.
Even if you say it is not,
Waving with the flowery wind,
It gets sick in its shame
By the red flower bud of a lotus.

꽃의 노래

찬 서리 맞은 돌 밑
얼어붙은 땅
마른 이끼 위엔
소름 돋아나고
엎드려 숨죽인 세월 지나
얼음 풀리는 날
잊었던 생각
실타래 풀리듯
다시 숨 쉬는 날에
순백의 날갯짓 하며
가까이 다가오는
그대 모습
경이롭다

솟아오른 연둣빛
화관모花冠帽 쓰고
풋풋한 생명줄
하늘로 솟구친다
수정궁에서
솟아오른 요정처럼

A Flower's Song

Under the cold frosted rock,
In the frozen land,
The goose flesh
Sprouts on the dry moss,
On the day of melting ice
After spending the tyrannized years,
And on the day we respire again
As if the thoughts we forgot
Unloose the tangled thread,
Your figure
Drawing near
Flapping on the sheer white wings
Is wondrous.

The fresh stalks
Of flower's life
With its light green crown on
Are soaring high in the sky.
You, god of beauty,
Like a rising nymph

그대 미의 사신이여
맑은 눈망울 꽃빛
가녀린 꽃술에
영혼의 다스림이
어여쁜 꽃잎에
입 맞추고
그대 미소 지으며
연분홍 깃발 흔든다

바람 속의 하얀 그리움

In the Crystal Palace,
The soul's managing
Over the weak pistils of clear eyes
Kissing its beautiful petals,
And you, smiling
Wave your pink flag.

봄날 詩의 몸짓 날아오르다

나는 웃고 있죠
왜죠
그냥 자꾸만 웃음이 나요

보세요, 저기
고요로운 언덕배기 위로
바람이 속살거리고 간 자리
은빛 햇살 너울 쓰고
내가 먼저 내가 먼저 하며
앞 다투어 불쑥불쑥 올라오는
아직은 젖은 눈망울을

보세요, 저기
개나리꽃 옆으로 날아가는 까치
꽁지에 노란 물 들었죠
산허리 감싸고 내려오는 온기에
마른 가지에서 연둣빛 속잎이
눈웃음 머금고 피어 오르죠

덩달아 시어詩語들 날개 달고 오르죠

A Poetic Gesture Flaps on the Wings in Spring Day

I laugh,
Why you?
Still, always I laugh.

Look at there
Over the silent hill,
Striving to be first in carelessly climbing up
To place the wind passed whispering,
In saying 'I, first of all, I, first'
With veiling the silver sunlight,

Look at there,
The tearful eyes yet,
And the magpie flying beside the golden bells,
Whose tail dyed in yellow colored.
The light green leaf's inside from the dry
  branch
By the warm air descending down through
  the hillside
Blooms out with having a smile on her eyes.

Following suit, the poetic words soar up on
  the wings.

목련, 바람 속의 하얀 그리움

그것은 바람 때문이 아니었다
영겁으로 이어진 간절한
그리움 때문이었을까
침묵으로 얼구어 낸 혼불의 화신이다

동짓달 그믐께까지 혹한의 서슬에도
별빛 고요로움 아래
냉기에 얼어붙은 나목으로 서서
삼동三冬 지날 때까지
미동도 없었거늘

꽃사슴 정기를 받아 꽃물 취하고
어디 님 찾아 백화의 면사포 드리우고
천상으로 오르려 했던가
황후의 기상으로
하얀 그리움의 화신으로 서 있다

The Magnolia, White Nostalgia on the Wind

It's not the reason of the wind's fault,
Or was it the reason of an ardent yearning,
Linked together by eternity?
It is an incarnation reclaimed from silence.

In spite of the sharp coldness until the
  coldest winter months
Under the silent starlight,
Standing as a naked tree frozen by coldness
Until passing the 3 months of winter,
It stood as firm as a rock,

It got its sap from a fawn's spirit
Hanging lover's white veil down,
And tried to ascend to the heaven?
Now in an empress's spirit
It stands as an incarnation of a white
  yearning.

II.

드림 소나타

Dream Sonata

꿈

만져지는가 하면
사라지는
오색 비눗방울
새벽이
오기 전까지의
밤이슬같이
겨울잠 속에
들어 있는 봄

A Dream

Five colored soap bubbles
Can be touched,
Or faded away,
Like a night dew
Till dawn comes,
Spring stays
Into winter's sleep.

샛강

별 노래를 따라 왔어요
바람이 등을 두드려
뒤돌아보다 길을 잃었어요
별 그림자조차 찾을 수가 없네요
여기 이끼 낀 사잇길에서
다리를 펴야겠어요
발끝을 간질이는 손길 멈추어 주세요
먼 길을 가야 하니
오늘밤은 징검다리를 베고
새우잠이라도 자 두어야겠어요
구름 이불 덮고 바다를 꿈꾸어요
풀잎이 소름처럼 돋네요
나팔꽃 귀 쫑긋 세우고
세상을 듣고 있어요
꿈꾸는 날은 터질 듯이
입술 위에 꽈리 부풀어 오르네요
내일 일을 생각하니
가슴에도 꽈리 부풀어 오르네요

A Tributary Stream

I came with a star's song.
A wind clapped me on the back, and
Looking back round, I lost my way.
Even a star's shadow I didn't find.
Here at the mossy byway
I have to stretch my legs.
Please, stop to tickle my tiptoe,
Because I have to go far.
Tonight I have to sleep curled up
With my head on the stepping stones
And I dream a sea with putting on the
  cloud-quilt.
The grass leaves sprout like goose flesh.
The trumpet-flowers with pricking up its
  ears,
Listen to this world.
The dreaming day swells up
Lips-rending like a blister above lips.
Thinking of tomorrow's plan,
My heart swells up like a blister.

커피 칸타타

사랑하는 이여 잠을 깨요
일어나 여기 날아간
새의 깃털 하나
귓가에 대어 보아요
바람이 스치고 간
자작나무 숲에서 들려오는
자작거리는 소리 들어 보아요
밤은 갈색의 짙은 계곡으로 들어가
사향의 은은한 향으로 번지네요
순백의 별빛이 은하에서 내려와
바흐의 G선상의 아리아를 타고
당신의 흐트러진 머리칼 사이로
흐르네요, 사랑하는 이여
우리의 사랑도 커피 잔에
뜨겁게 내리잖아요
이 밤의 감미로운 커피를 즐겨요
우리의 달콤한 입맞춤이 식기 전에

바람 속의 하얀 그리움

The Coffee Cantata

O Sweet heart, wake up yourself from sleep,
Get up and put one feather of a bird
To your ears,
That has been blown away.
Please, listen to the sound of a white birch
Falling on my ears from the birch wood
Which a wind passed.
The night enters the deep brown valley,
And spreads with a soft aroma of musk.
The pure white starlight comes down from
  the Milky Way
On the air of G-string's Aria of Bach,
Flows between your scattered hairs.
My beloved,
Our love falls down as hot as in coffee cup.
Enjoy the sweet coffee on this night
Before our sweetish kiss gets cold.

사랑이 흐르는 빛

당신의 웃음소리
폭죽 터지듯
하늘 길 가르며
별빛처럼 올라가고

그 소리 부채처럼 펼쳐져
햇살 가루되어
눈부시게 쏟아지네

그 햇살 물살이 되어
내 뼈骨 길 사이사이로
밀물처럼 들어와

그 물살 봄비 되어
내 영혼까지 적시네

마흔 번이나 각인된 나이테
세월이 앉았다 간 자국으로
이제는 희미해졌지만

The Light Streaming with Love

Your laugh,
As if it sets off firecrackers,
Ascends like star's light,
Cleaving the heaven's way,

Its sound that is spread like fan
Making rays of light into powder,
Pours down splendidly.

The sun-rays forming a flow like water,
Through my bone's ways
Come in like the tide,

The current flow of water as spring-rains
Also gets my soul wet.

Though the annual ring carved forty times
As the trace of years,
Seems vague now,

아직도 나는 그 빛으로
당신의 그림자 안에서
날마다 눈이 부십니다

바람 속의 하얀 그리움

Still by the light
In the your shadow
My eyes are dazzling everyday.

색동저고리

시집 올 때 데리고 온 그녀
내실 깊은 요람에서 출입 끊은 채
공주병 걸린 듯 고운 잠만 잔다
흐르는 세월에 잊혀진 그녀가 생각나
장롱 깊은 서랍 열고 들여다보면
나비처럼 곱게 날개 접고
새아씨 첫날밤인 양 초승달 눈 감은 채
고요히 햇살 미소 머금고 잠만 잔다
규중閨中의 얌전한 모습으로
연두색 명주양단 저고리 색동 깃 고름
목선 어깨에 붙여진 반달 색동 팔소매
땟물 묻지 않은
연한 순 솜털이 상긋한 분 내음
순결한 모습 그대로다
바깥바람 맞지 않은 그녀는
세월의 흔적도 상처도 없다
어머니가 채워주신 따스한 온기를 품고

A Rainbow-Striped Jacket

When I get married to a man taking her along,
Who could not go in and out freely from a deep
   cradle in the main room,
Only sleep gracefully as if she gets sick in
  'princess to be.'
Thinking of her, slipped my mind from the long years,
I opened a deep wardrobe's drawer to see in,
Finding only to sleep with her wings folded like
   a butterfly,
With her thread eyes closed as a new lady,
And with having a bright smile on her lips.
A graceful figure of a boudoir,
The light green garment of silk satin with its
   colored coat string,
And a colored half moon-like sleeve attached to
   her slender neck
And the tender down with no grime has fresh smell,
These pure looks are just what she had.
She, being constant,
Has no scar and wound of years.
She is so kind

보이지 않는 곳에서
늘 나를 지켜주는 고마운 그녀

바람 속의 하얀 그리움

Enough to keep me out of sight,
With warm mind given from my mother.

詩낭송회에 가면

詩낭송회에 가면
그곳은 질박한 시루다
굽고 말리고
아홉 번 중탕해도 좋다
떡 하듯 시루에 찌고 또 쪄서
잘 뜸 들여 내놓은 시어들이
훈김으로 뿌옇게 솟아오른다

詩낭송회에 가면
그곳은 물 맑은 어항이다
물고기처럼 팔팔한 시어詩語들
싱싱하게 살아서 물보라친다
금빛 은빛 반짝이는 비늘
유연한 지느러미 살랑인다

詩낭송회에 가면
그곳은 단옷날

Going to the Meeting of Reciting Poems

Going to the meeting for reciting poems,
In which we had better warm up it,
Bake it, and make dry in a plain earthenware
  steamer
In a double boiler, even 9 times.
Steaming it and heating up as we steam
  rice-cakes in the earthenware steamer,
The poetic words given enough time,
Rise up hazily in warm air.

The meeting for reciting poems we go to
Is like a clear goldfish basin.
The fresh poetic words like fishes
Raise spray as being alive,
Their scales glitter in a silvery and golden colors,
And their flexible fins wag softly.

Reading poems at the meeting for reciting poems
Is the same as a swing tied up under the a
  willow

버드나무 아래 매인 그네다

연분홍 치맛자락 그네 타듯

너울너울 하늘 길 가른다

옥 비취 대님 끈

시향詩香타고 출렁인다

In Dano* Festival.

The light pink skirt trails sitting on a swing,

Estrange the earth from the heaven wavingly,

And the pent-leg ties of green jade

Roll on the poetic aroma.

* *Dano* Festival: It's a kind of traditional Korean festival on the fifth day of the fifth lunar month(5th, May).

열대야

아흔아홉 칸 열두 대문 모두 열어놓아도
바람은 줄행랑치고 어디 납작 엎드렸을까
온종일 해님과의 기氣싸움에 밀려났나
온몸 비비꼬더니 털끝 하나 안 보인다
장독대 휘둘러 나온 수원 댁의 치맛자락
갈지之자 걸음에 그림자 출렁이고
이마주름 사이로 여름 달빛이 하얗다
기운차던 매미소리도 뒷동산 푸른 물소리도
간헐적으로 들리는 웃음소리에 주춤댄다
구름도 멈춰 서서 귀 기울이면
뒷목에서 젖어 나온 땀으로 온몸은 스멀대고
곳곳의 세포마저 입 벌리고 하품하는 밤
백일홍 붉은 꽃잎도 조는 듯 힘이 없다
어디서 백합화 향 한 줄기 생수를 부어준다
무릎 위의 아이는 어느새 잠이 들고
부채질 간간이 이어지는 여름밤은 그렇게

* the zigzag step: It means the step in a shape like the
chinese character 之.

A Tropical Night

Though opened 12 gates of 99 rooms,
A wind ran away, where did it lie flat?
Or did it be pushed from a seesaw struggle with
the sun all day?
Twisting its body about it disappears out of sight.
Mrs. Suwon's skirt's trouser coming out from the terrace
To keep jars of soy sauce, surges as its shadow of
the zigzag* step,
And the summer moonlight shines whitely
between her forehead's wrinkles.
The cicada's energetic sound and the blue water's
sound in behind the hill
Waver in intermittent laughing sound.
The floating clouds stop to hear them(the sounds),
The whole body is felt crawly in sweating from
the behind neck.
In the night that even every cell yawns,
When the red crape-myrtle's petal has no energy
as dozing,
A strand of a lily blossom's fragrance pours like
living water.
The meteors fall from the far heaven,
The baby on my lap falls asleep,
So does the summer night in the fanning at times.

뜨거운 밤

68억 세계인이 잠 못 드는 밤
가슴마다 번개 치며 불이 붙는다
세계축구의 한가운데 말뚝 박고 선 태극전사
16강 문턱을 넘어 행복의 도가니에 꿈을 싣고
8강의 진입로에서 꿈을 터트린다
절묘한 한 꼴이 밤을 뜨겁게 달구고
요하네스버그의 밤은 타는 듯 깊어간다
붉은 악마의 물결 붉은 파도로 넘실거리고
응원자들 어깨는 흔들흔들 엉덩이는 들썩들썩
하늘에 꽃불을 그리며 튀는
공격수와 수비수가 날리는 공
아슬아슬한 장면에 숨이 막힌다
공이 튀는 순간 마다
기쁜 마음 아픈 가슴 엇갈리고
응원의 함성은 넘치는 감격으로
모르는 사람도 부둥켜안고 몸부림친다
아 골대에 입 맞추고 비껴가는

바람 속의 하얀 그리움

A Hot Night

The night 68 thousand millions of world
  people fail to get asleep,
Lightning flashes and catches on fire in
  every bosom.
The Korean players, taking a place in the
  center of the world football,
Load our dreams in a crucible of happiness,
And are about to get a dream's goal at an
  entrance of 8 nation's tournament.
One fine goal, making this night hot
Johannesburg's night grows late like excitement.
"The red devil's wave" surges as red billows,
And the cheerer's shoulders sway and their
  rumps are restless,
The attacking and defensive players' ball
Flies in the air as a heaven's flame,
So the narrow scenes of both sides are choked.
At every ball's bound
Both joy and grief alternate in both breasts,
The rooter's shouting in the over-passion
  makes even on-lookers hug and struggle in joy.
Ah, like the destiny's goddess,

운명의 여신 치맛자락

붙잡지 못하고 사라지는 그림자에

쏟아지는 눈물 그라운드를 적시고

뜨거운 강줄기 되어 흐른다

다시 또 4년을 꿈꾸며 눈물을 먹는다

뜨거운 밤은 유성처럼 흐르고

석패惜敗의 구장엔 'G세대'의 싹이 돋는다

The ball kissing at the gall post and passing
  over it,
Both sides fail to get the chance,
At the disappearing shadow of victory,
Their shedding tears drench the ground,
And flows in a great river.
Lots of people wait for 4 years again repressing
  their tears,
And he hot night flows so as the falling star,
At the ground of the defeat by a narrow margin
The bud of 'G-generation' sprouts again.

손톱 속 유영遊泳

내 손톱 안엔 작은 우주가 있다
무음의 힐링 열차 지나간 자리엔
빛바랜 하현달이 아스라하다
꿈꾸고 있는지 몽롱하다
나는 별자리에 서서
행성으로 가는 별꽃 길을 바라본다
홀로 인증 샷하고 돌아선 자리
머리에 꽂고 간 나비 핀 하나
연분홍 날개 펴고 날아오른다
이어서 한 마리 또 한 마리
수많은 나비들이 부화한다
푸른 하늘을 덮고 우주로의 도킹
블랙홀로 빨려가는 길이다
지구의 오염이 아직 침해되지 않은
은하수 밭 바람재 너머엔
소금밭이 보석처럼 뿌려져 있다
꽃불 든 작은 들풀의 향연이다

바람 속의 하얀 그리움

Swimming in Nail

There is a little universe in my finger nail,
And a waning clouded moon hangs far-off
On the spot the soundless healing train passed over,
All things seem to be loomed in dreaming.
Standing on the lane of star-flowers
Going from lots of star constellations to the permanent
  one, In the place I have certified alone and returned.
A butterfly hairpin stuck in my head
Soars up spreading its soft pink wings.
Then, one head, again one head, and
Lots of butterflies are hatched out.
They cover the blue sky, and flying for
  docking to the universe
Being absorbed into Black Hole.
Over the windy hill filed of Galaxy,
The slat field that has not been polluted by
  the earth,
Is scattered like jewels.
It's a festival of small field grasses with a
  flaming fire.

오래된 겨울 꿈

"평창!"
남아공 더반을 울린 이 한마디
정적을 깨고 불꽃이 튄다
십이 년 오랜 겨울 꿈이
홰를 치며 날아오른다

그것은 긴 염원이었다
무너질 수 없는 신념이었다

"예스 평창"
2018년을 향한
승리의 날개 달고 동계올림픽의
'새로운 지평'이 열리는
이 밤,
기쁨에 잠 못 드는 대한민국
강원도의 회한의 눈물이
감격의 눈물로 역류하여 흐른다
급물살 타고 지구촌으로
퍼져나가는 승리의 웃음소리

A Long Winter Dream

"Yes, Pyeong-chang!"
A word that rang from Durban of the Republic
of South Africa,
Breaks the silence and sparks the flame.
A long dream of 12 years
Flaps its wings and soars in the air.

It was a long heart's desire
It was an unshaken conviction.

"Yes, Peong-chang"
This night,
In which 'A new Horizon of the Winter Olympic'
Will open on the wings of victory
Toward the year, 2018.
In this night Koreans fail to go sleep a wink all night,
The regrettable tears of Gangwon-do people
Flows in an adverse tide as deep emotional ones.
The laughing sound of victory
Spreads out to the global town on the rapid current,
Many people clap their hands,

긴 악몽 벗고 박수 터지고 목 터진다
대한민국이 행복한 밤이다

And raise their voice loudly with a long
  nightmare left behind.
It's a happy night of Korea,

겨울 숲엔 아직 꿈이

우기 지나고
강설降雪 그친 지 오랜
겨울 숲으로 간다
태양은 금빛 월계관을 벗고
새로운 설계도를 그리기 위해 돌아갔나
별도 달도 은빛 날개를 접고
구름 그늘 뒤로 몸을 감추었다
구름도 무심히 지나치는 하늘
그 아래 노랫소리 그친 지 오래거늘
천고의 꿈은 침묵으로 덮이어
겨울 숲은 고요 적막이 흐른다
밤 깊을수록 시심詩心도 깊어지고
불면이 아닌 혹한의 칼날
싹을 틔우고 꽃을 피우기 위해
스스로 몸부림치고 정화하여
다시 일어서기 위해 안간힘 쓴다
고독과 싸우고 있나
산등성이 골짜기 숲 후미진 곳 잔설
포옹을 풀고 실눈 뜨는데

겨울 숲은
아직도 꿈꾸고 있는가

Still a Dream in the Winter Wood

I go to the winter wood,
That the rainy season passed
And the snowfall stopped long ago.
Did the sun go back to make a new plan
With its laurel crown putting off?
The stars and moon folded their golden wings,
And hid themselves behind the cloud's shadow.
The sky that the clouds passed by heedlessly,
Under which the songs had stopped long time ago,
The unchangeable dream was covered with silence,
And the winter wood is lonesome in calmness.
The later it grows at night, the deeper the poetic mind is,
And on the coldest day, not in insomnia,
In order to sprout, and bloom a flower,
It struggles and purifies itself,
And holds back an urge to rise again.
Is it fighting with loneliness
The lingering snow in the secluded place of the
   winter hill
Narrows its eyes with its dress put off,

The winter wood
Dreams still a dream?

마지막 잎새를 위한 연가

달력 한 장,
오 헨리의 '마지막 잎새' 되어
거실 벽에 희망으로 붙어 있다
일 년 동안 날마다
제 살 한 점씩 떼어주며
우리 집안의 대소사를 챙겼지
아침엔 창으로의 은빛 햇살을 받으며
고운 눈웃음 풀어 넣고
새 날을 꿈꾸라 하였는데
붉은색 볼펜으로
날짜에 동그라미 쳐 놓으면
꽃으로 피어나 꽃밭 일구어 주고
창으로 들어온 바람 타면서
꿈 물결치며 노래 불렀지
한 가닥씩 함께 맞들고 온 날들인데
이제는 대망을 품으라 하며
아낌없이 한 점 남은 살점마저
떼어주고 떠나는 뒷모습
머물렀던 자리엔 새 희망이 걸려 있다

A Love Song for the Last Leaf

A piece of the calendar,
Hangs on the living room's wall as a hope
Like 'a last leaf' of O Henry.
Every day for one year,
It tears off a drop of its own flesh,
And has put many things of my house in order.
The leaf, receiving the silvery sunshine from
  windows in the morning,
Untied its pretty smile,
And made me dream a new day,
So if I drew a circle on the day in red
  ball-pen,
It bloomed as a flower clearing the flower
  bed,
And I sung a song on waves of dream
With winds from windows.
They are days lifting up together one by one,
Saying to me, "cherish a great hope",
From your looks behind, leaving me and
Tearing off even the last flesh unsparingly,
Another hope hangs on the remained place.

Ⅲ.

물음표 소고小考

A Little Thought on the Question Mark

은빛 명상

밤으로의 긴 여로
침묵의 대행진이
펼쳐놓고 간 은반
계명성 은빛 내린 자국마다
삶의 검은 눈동자 굴러간다

이팝꽃 허물 벗은 자리
하얀 깃발 꽂아 놓고
낮달 기다리는데

어디서 날아온 빠알간
단풍잎 한 장
나비처럼 사뿐히 앉아
수묵화를 그리는 설야

바람 속의 하얀 그리움

A Silver Meditation

A long journey for the night,
A silver plate that the great parade of silence
Has spread, and the black eyes of life
On every silver mark of Venus
Are rolling.

The spot that Chionanthus* cast off its skin,
Sticking the white banner,
And waiting a moon at noon,

A sheet of red maple leaf
Wavering from somewhere,
Sits softly as a butterfly,
And are drawing India ink-picture on snowing
    night.

---

* A genus of low trees or shrubs having drooping panicles of
  fragrant flowers with   narrow petals.

자작나무 나목 숲

그 숲엔
은빛 강 흐르고
맑고 투명하여
온 겨우내
눈이 시리다

하얗게 벗은
나목 위로
차가운 달빛
투영하니
순백의 향기
영혼을 감싼다

바람 속의 하얀 그리움

The Wood of the Naked White Birch

In the wood
The silvery river flows,
And it's clear and crystal
All through winter,
It's for us to be dazzling.

Above the naked tree,
Undressed whitely
A cold moonlight
Is projected,
Its sheer snow-white aroma
Covers our soul.

담쟁이 생존방식

스스로 깨달아
구도의 길에 이르듯이
언제 태어날 때부터
삶의 방식을 터득하였을까
석면의 냉기를 먹고도
존재에 빛을 발하며
동행자와 아울러
폐쇄회로를 빠져나와
천지를 품는 너는

An Ivy's Survival for Existence

How did you grasp the way for existence,
From your birth,
As if we seek after truth,
Ourselves realizing?
Drinking an asbestus's coldness,
And emanating being's light
With a companion,
Slipping out of the closing a circuit,
You, holding heaven and earth in your
   bosom.

아파트 춘

길고 짧은
이야기를
가슴에 켜켜이
담고 있는
인간시장
대하소설이다
아직도
끝나지 않은
연속극이다

An Apartment's Town

It's the market of human beings,
A saga novel,
Containing
A long and short
Story
In their heart in several layers.
And it's not ended
Yet,
But it's a serial drama.

메타포를 찾아

너는 나의 끝없는 목마름
어느 미로의 길에서
시간의 모래알갱이
그 모래시계 속으로 들어가
정체성을 찾아 헤매다
미아가 되는구나
물안개에 빠져 허우적거리다
지친 날갯죽지 내리고
허기져 돌아오는 길엔
한 알 물방울이 되어
빈 망태기 둘러메고 오누나
허공을 딛는 발자국 따라오는
죽녹원의 댓잎 소리
바람을 비끼는구나

바람 속의 하얀 그리움

In Search of Metaphor

You are an endless thirst of mine,
The sands of time
In any way of a labyrinth
Enter a sandglass,
Searching for the original form,
And gets lost.
Pawing the air to get out of the water-fog
With their tired wings folded,
On their way home felt hungry,
Return with an empty bag on shoulders
As a drop of waterdrop.
The sound of reed's leaves in the field of reeds
Following up the footsteps in the empty air
Is slanting a wind.

물음표 소고小考

진한 잉크색 바닷물 쿡 찍어
획을 내리 긋다 잃어버린 길
막힌 길에서 손에 잡은 붓대
방향키를 돌려 본다
너무 직선으로만 내달렸나
물음표 낚아 올리자
바람이 일어나
휑하니 채우지 못한
빈 가슴에 머문다
바람의 끝을 잡아 본다
막힌 담이 무너지고
수많은 별들의 세계에 묻혔다
언제 은하계로 들어왔을까
은빛 갈대 바람에 부대끼면서
내 앞으로 쏠려온다
갈대밭 미로 속 헤집고 나와
손에 쥔 것을 보니
물음표는 어디 가고
은발의 갈대 한 잎 뿐

　　바람 속의 하얀 그리움

A Little Thought on the Question Mark

The lost way,
Dipping the pen into deep ink colored seawater,
Making a stroke, from the blocked way
I turn the direction key as a brush handle in my hands.
Do I go too ahead of others?
As soon as I angle a question mark up,
A wind begins to blow
And stays in my empty heart,
In which I has not filled desertedly.
I catch the end of the wind,
The blocked wall fell down,
And buried in the world of lots of stars.
When did it go into the Milky Way?
Running against the wind of the silver reed,
It presses on me.
After I got over the labyrinth of the reed's field,
Only I found in my hands
A piece of leaf of the silver reed in my hand,
With no question mark.

옷장

하얀 성 안엔
마른 날개들이 모로 누워 있다
빛이 없어도
자기만의 빛깔을 지닌 채
기다림의 미학에 길들여져 있다
절망보다는
꿈을 품고 날아가고 싶겠지
울음소리는
입속의 사탕처럼 달콤한 미소에
녹아 허공을 우주로 삼는다
하얀 햇살이
분무처럼 쏟아져 들어갈 때면
정으로 맞물려 있는
고요로운 요람에서 날고 싶겠지
솟구쳐 날아올라
실크로드를 찾아 가 보려나
번화가 군중 틈에
날갯짓하며 빛을 발하고 싶겠지

A Wardrobe

In the white castle
The dry wings lie on one's side.
Without a light,
Only with their own color,
They got accustomed to esthetics of expectation.
Perhaps they are willing to fly embracing a
  dream
Instead of despair.
Their crying sound
Is melted by a delicious smile,
Makes an empty void as a cosmos.
When the white sunshine
Pours in atomizing,
They would like to fly at the silent cradle
Coming in contact with emotion.
Are they willing to soar up
In search for the silk-road?
Perhaps they want to emit the light
Flapping their wings between crowds of
  business quarters.

손금에서 길을 찾다

무심히 펼쳐본 손바닥
무수한 길이
노란 별 눈을 달고 달린다
끝 간 데 모를 제 길을 잘도 달린다
생명의 길로 달리는 직진선에서
잠시 쉬어갈까 쉼표 하나 찍는다
유턴으로 돌아오는 회향 길에서
사유의 바다에 빠져
유년의 찰나적 멈춤을
곡선의 탐미적 시각이 환상을 꿈꾼다
어느 행성으로의 진입로를 찾고 있나
창 너머 유리창 밖을 내려다본다
구름의 망각 그늘에 드리운 검은 도로
빨갛게 충혈된 눈을 흘기며
거북이 등처럼 굽은 등을 한 차들이
꼬리를 물고 시간을 곰삭이고 서 있다
바늘귀 더듬으며 찾아가는 길이다
저마다 가야 할 진입로를 찾아
믿음의 더듬이를 들이대고 있다

Searching for the Way of the Palm's Lines

A lot of ways
Which I spread my palm casually,
Are running with yellow star's eyes,
And are running the boundless way of their
  own very well.
I imprint a pause at the straight line
Running for the way of life to rest for a moment.
In the way returning in U-turn
Sunk into the sea of thought,
I dream a fantasy in an esthetic view of curved lines
Through a momentary suspension of infancy
Do we search for an access road of any planet?
I look down outside over the window.
In the black road, suspended in the shadow
  of cloud's retina
Leering with their red bloodshot eyes,
The cars with the turtle's back
Are stopping bumper to bumper,
Killing time, and so hard way as to look for
  a needle's eye.
We are using an antenna of our belief,
Searching for the access road heading for our
  own way.

종소리

자각의 날선 끝이 폐부를 찌른다
황막한 어둠의 청동 못에서
응집凝集된 자존의 상실감은 용해되어
석류수로 흘러내려 물이 되어 흐를까
흐르다 맑디맑은 청정의 계곡에 이르러
서른세 번 재계齋戒하면
옷깃의 먼지는 바람 되어 날아갈까
푸르디푸른 함성으로
산 숲 바람벽에서 숨을 고르고
욕심이 웅크리고 있는 거리를 건너 뛴다
어디를 갈까 머물 곳 찾지 못하고
늦가을 맑은 햇빛 아래 맴도는 고추잠자리
한 쪽 날개 끝 어디에 상처 입고
실핏줄 터진 모세혈관
은사 실로 짜여진 곱디고운 날개
지문처럼 남아 있는 상흔은
외치는 소리 빈 껍질 허물로만 남겨놓고

바람 속의 하얀 그리움

A Sound of the Bell

A keen edge of self-consciousness stabs the
  vital point.
In the bronze pond of the waste darkness
The forfeiture of cohesive self-respect is
  dissolved
As garnet, flowing as water?
If it reaches the clearest valley of purity
And performs 33 times of ablutions,
Could dusts of clothes fly in a wind?
In a great outcry
It takes breath at the wall of the mountain's
  wood,
Runs across the street curled up with desire.
Where does it go? Not looking for the place
  to stay,
A red dragonfly spinning itself
Under the clear sunshine in the late autumn,
With one wing's end of wings being injured,
A capillary tube splits open.
The scars, remained like a fingerprint
On the beautiful wings woven with silver thread,

어디 모를 곳으로 바람으로 날아 갔나
다시는 되돌아올 리 없는 흐름이라도

명경지수로 흐르고 또 흐르리

Left behind only as an empty shell in spite
   of its shouting,
Did it fly to the place as a wind nobody knows?
Even if it is a flow of no return again,
It would flow and flow as clear as a looking glass.

바람의 후유증

태풍 곤파스가 할퀴고 간 자리
다시 또 물 폭탄 세례 쏟아진 산자락엔
죽은 침묵의 언어들이 나뒹굴고 있다
우람한 나무들 한순간에 요절나고
날벼락 맞아 밑동까지 뒤집혀서
아름드리 큰 기둥이 회오리치던 바람에
가위표로 포개져 있다 오, 안 돼!
신념은 무너지고 하늘을 등지고 엎어졌다
뿌리째 몽땅 뽑혀진 위로 내리 비치는 햇살
마지막 수분까지 빼앗기고 숨을 헐떡인다
껍질이 찍혀 벗겨 올라간 몸통
치맛자락 젖혀진 여인의 속살같이 드러나고
물굽이 소용돌이칠 때마다
휩쓸린 나뭇잎 파편들 파르라니 떨고 있다
휑하니 거친 바람이 살을 에이고 스쳐 지나간다
쓰러진 거목 아래 드러난 붉은 흙 속엔
달개비꽃 하나 파랗게 질려
가녀린 날개 쳐들고 하늘을 본다

바람 속의 하얀 그리움

The Aftermath of Wind

In the traces that the typhoon, 'Gonpas' scratched,
And again in the mountain side it poured the
    water-bomb,
The dead languages of silence are rolling over.
The big trees are destroyed in a moment,
And the lower parts of them are turned
    inside out by a sudden calamity,
The big posts of them are overlapped
One another by the whirlwind, O, no!
The self-reliance collapses, against a heaven,
And the sunlight shines down over trees
    taken out with their roots,
They pant with last moisture deprived of.
Their barks are peeled upwardly,
So their body are disclosed like an inner
    part of the woman's dress,
At every swirling torrents
The broken pieces of trees are trembling with cold.
In the red soil disclosed under the fallen big tree,
One of the
Dalgaebee* flower is turned deadly pale with horror,
Looks up the sky, lifting up her poor wings.

---

* Dalgaebee flower : It looks like an ornament of
   cock-head like field grass.

IV.

여행 스케치

Travelling Sketches

꿈꾸는 날개

떠날 날 아직인데
손길은 쥐방울 드나들 듯
넣고 빼고 빼고 넣고
여행가방 열고 닫기
분주하기만 하다
손마디와 가방 문
한 옥타브 넘어선 음계
불협화음 연발해도
초침은 모르는 채 비켜간다

마음속 곱게 접어놓은
꿈꾸던 노랑 날개 펴고
먼 나라 낯선 도시
햇빛 쏟아지는 거리
이국의 모르는 사람
틈길 활보하면서
삶의 활력소 유쾌한 웃음소리
새 청사진도 담아온다
떠날 때 설레던 마음
보금자리 온기 식기 전
돌아올 땐 더욱 들뜬다

The Dreaming Wings

The day to depart is still far,
My hands are so busy
Enough to put them and pull them,
Again pulling and putting them,
Several times as opening and closing a luggage
The knuckle and the bag's door,
As a scale raising an octave
Even it is discordant repeatedly,
The second hand of a watch passes by involuntarily.

With yellow wings spread
I have dreamed beautifully into the heart,
Striding along the byway
Between the unfamiliar city of the far country,
The street with glaring sunlight,
And unknown people of different countries,
I come, with a cheerful laugh of a tonic life,
And a new blueprint.
The throbbing mind when I leave,
Before the warmth of a nest gets cold,
When coming back, my mind grows restless more.

런던 아이

뉴 밀레니엄 기념으로
세워진 회전 구조물
거대한 바퀴 하나
템즈 강을 발로 차고
큰 물고기처럼 솟아오른다
하얀 햇빛에 물든
반짝이는 은빛 굴렁쇠
물레방아처럼 돌아간다
긴 꼬리 줄을 만든 사람들
누가 지우개로 지웠는지
눈 깜짝 사이 지워지고
바퀴 끝에 매달려 있는
투명 유리 캡슐 속으로
빨려 들어간다
다람쥐 쳇바퀴 돌 듯
삼백육십 도 돌아가며
발끝에 펼쳐진 도시의 강과
시가지와 풍경을 먹으며
강 빛 속에 잠긴다

London's Eye

One huge wheel of the turning framework,
Built in the memory of the new millenium,
Kicks the Thames,
And soars up like a big fish.
The silver shining hoop,
That is dyed in the sunlight
Rolls like a water-mill.
As if someone erased by a eraser
People who made a long line,
Their line is erased in a blink,
And is sucked up
Into the crystal capsule
Hanging on the end of the wheel.
Turning round in 360 degrees
As a squirrel turns the frame of a sieve,
They sink in the light of the river,
Enjoying by eyes the river of the city,
Its streets and a landscape
Stretched under the feet.

고도古都에 꽃비 내리다

고색古色으로 물들었네
창연蒼然한 이 도시
태고의 신비로움이 미소로 흐르네
낯 설음 오히려 정겨웁고
지나는 이 없어도
바람은 잠자는 꽃가지
흔들어 깨우네
꽃잎 낱알 흩날리는 꽃보라
꽃비에 젖으며 걷는 나그네
부서지는 햇살가루에 눈 시리고
꽃향기에 취해 발걸음 더디네
아, 환희로 차오르는 이 마음
신이 주시는 선물인가
어디쯤 천국으로의 계단이
나타날 것 같은 이 고도古都
몇 천 년 지나는 흐름에도
밀려오는 꽃 향은 언제나
옛 이야기 갈무리하고
더 깊은 세월의 뿌리를 내리네

바람 속의 하얀 그리움

The Flowery Rain Falls in the Ancient City

This ancient city
Is dyed gloomy,
Flows with mystic smile of immemorial time.
An unfamiliarity is rather affectionate,
Even without passersby
The wind awakens sleeping twigs.
The wayfarers walk getting wet in the flowery rain
With scattering flower-storm of flower petals,
Feeling sore for eyes because of pollen in sunshine,
So they are slow of foot being drunken of the
    flower's aroma.
Ah, my heart, overflowing with joy,
Is this a present given from God?
This is the antiquated city
That the stairs for the kingdom of heaven
Are likely to appear before us.
In spite of thousand of years passed,
The pouring fragrance,
Always putting the old stories in order,
Takes root deeper in the years.

고성古城에 오르다

- 스코틀랜드 에딘버러 캐슬

천년 시간 틈새에 끼어 바라본다
타임머신 타고 와 되돌린 듯
나 서 있는 곳 중세의 도시 아닌가
도시 한가운데 절벽으로
깎아 세운 돌 성
희뿌연 비린 안개비에 젖어
마법의 성처럼 잿빛으로 덮여 있다
무겁게 눈꼬리 하늘에 걸고
두 팔 벌려 땅금 긋고 서서
치열했던 싸움터의 흔적을 일깨운다
꼭대기 성곽 따라 박아놓은 대포
요새를 지키기 위해 불을 토했어도
죽음으로 흘린 피는
화약 냄새에 젖어 바다로 흘러갔을 뿐
디지털 시대로 달려온 역사를 읽으며
바람은 늙지도 않은 채 서성거린다

Climbing an Antique Castle

- Edinburgh Castle, Scotland

I look at it through the gap of thousands of time,
As if returning here in time machine,
Isn't a medieval city where I stand?
The castle, built of the cut stones,
On the cliff of the middle of the city,
In the gray fogged rain
Is covered with gray color like a magic castle.
The castle, with its heavy eye-tail hung on
   the sky,
Situating to draw line with its two hands
   stretched,
Makes us aware of the scars of the fierce
   fighting site.
The cannons, fixed along the top-castle,
Even fired in order to keep the fortress,
But the shedding blood of death
Flew only to the sea with smell of the gunpowder,
The wind with no age limit
Stagers reading the story of the digital age,
And the bagpipe's song with roaring sounds

지구촌 관광 오가는 발걸음 사이로
백파이프 소리 은은히

맴도는 넋의 위로를 가원하는 듯

Seems to consol the souls hanging about
Between steps of the sightseers
Coming and going from all global countries.

몽마르트 언덕

그 언덕에 다시 또 가보고 싶다
한낮의 태양이 눈이 시리게 쏘아대도
그 햇살 사이로 비집고 들어가
웃음을 되 쏘아대는 젊은 연인들의 양지
저 아래 세느강에서 깃털 내리고
조용히 올라오던 바람이 갑자기 귓발 쫑긋
할 말이 생각났나 보다
파리지앤느*의 금발을 흩뜨러 놓으며
한바탕 피카소의 붓 살인 양 내리치더니
변덕이 났나보다 바람은 고운 잠속에 들고
언덕에 늘어선 화폭 속 인물은 눈을 뜬다
누군가의 얼굴이 가난한 예술가의 혼을 담고
붓끝에서 화판으로 옮겨질 때
멋진 풍경화는 어느새 매무새 고쳐 잡고
물감 통에서 낭만으로 흐른다
샤크레쾌르 성당 계단에 앉아 있는 사람들
꽃무리 지으며 언어의 깃발 곧추세우는데

바람 속의 하얀 그리움

The Hill of Monmartre

I want to go the hill of Montmartre again.
Even though the sunlight at high noon is too
    dazzling to open eyes,
Squeezing oneself in between the sunbeams,
And folding its feather under the Seine river,
The sunny garden of the youngsters,
Who send a laugh, and the wind that rises up
    silently, suddenly cocking the ears,
Seems to remind itself to say something.
Shaking loose Parisienne* golden hair,
And making a blow hard like a brush handle of Picasso,
The wind, it may behave capriciously, fall into
    silent sleep,
The persons in canvases on the hill open their eyes.
When someone's face is contained with an
    artist's soul,
And is moved from the brush to the canvas,
The fine painting of landscape at once adjusts
    itself
And already the dye-stuffs box becomes romantic.
The people sitting on the stairs of the
Catholic church, Chaklequerre
With making beautiful groups and lifting up

파리 시내 에펠탑 찾아보는 눈길 사이로
오가는 이야기 끝없이 바람에 감긴다

* 파리지엔느 : 파리 여성

바람 속의 하얀 그리움

straight their banner of language,
Their stories between eyes looking for the Eiffel Tower,
Moves endlessly on the wing of a wind.

* parisienne : It means women of Paris in French.

디즈니월드

낯선 땅, 설레는 손놀림으로
17시간 비행의 짐을 풀어놓을 때
굳었던 마음 정감으로 풀어지고
도시의 뜨거운 숨결을 마신다

하늘엔 구름꽃 땅엔 웃음꽃
호반의 수중기가 열기를 식히지만
사람들의 정열만은 식히지 못하는 곳
이곳에선 이방인이란 없다
인파에 흘러가며 다인종 무리에 끼어
존재감에 충만한 자유인
앞서 가는 연인들이여,
흥겹게 들썩이는 어깨의 날갯짓
투스텝으로 가볍게 걸어가는 걸음걸이
그 사랑 영원하라 축복하는 마음
어느새 우리도 손잡고 마주본다

도시는 축포에 출렁이고
불꽃으로 휘몰아친다

The Disney World

When I, at strange land, with throbbing mind
Undo the baggages of 17 hour's flight,
The anxious mind is released with warm emotion,
And I respire the hot respiration of the city.

The flower of clouds in the sky, the one of
    laughs in the earth,
And vapours of the lake cool off hot weather,
But they don't cool our passion off here.
So there's no alien in this place.
We are all free men being replete with
    existential soul,
Who are flowing with groups mixed as various
    races.
Lovers, preceding before us,
Be forever for the lovable gestures of their
    exciting shoulder's shake,
Couple's walking lightly step by step,
Soon with our blessing mind,

The city waves with a cannon salute,
And was embroidered on fireworks.
We look at each other face to face in hands.

밤하늘에 퍼지는 꽃 타래
디즈니월드의 밤은
불꽃으로 덮여 꽃보다 아름다운
불꽃밭이다

바람 속의 하얀 그리움

The night's firework of the Disney World
With the floral design spreading into the sky on night,
Makes more beautiful garden of the firework's night
Than the blossom.

파라오 투탕카멘

눈길 닿는 곳마다 빛 부신
황금빛은 신비스럽다
이집트 왕들의 계곡에서 발굴한
투탕카멘 황금 마스크와 유물
찬탄의 한숨 출렁인다
삼천 년 흙속에 묻혔어도
변색되지 않고 살아 숨 쉬는 듯
생동하는 눈빛에 숨이 멎는다
그 찬란한 금빛으로도
속내에 드리운 어둠의 그림자는
지우지 못하였나 보다
황금판 그림문자는 꽃물결로 무늬지고
이마에 달고 있는 독수리와 코부라는
다가갈 수 없는 힘을 보여준다
죽어서도 놓치지 않으려고
안간힘 쓰는 두 손 안에 움켜진 왕권
해가 질 때부터 떠오를 때까지

Pharaoh's Tutankhamen

Its golden light is so mysterious,
As far as our eyes can reach.
The golden Tutankhamen Mask and relics
Excavated in the Egypt King's valley,
Make us admire for them.
Though buried into soil for 3 thousands years,
Its animating eye color as fast or alive as
  real gold
Almost makes us stop our breath.
However, the shadow of darkness suspended
  in its inside
Might be not erased even by the brilliant
  golden colors.
The golden pictures of figures are embroidered
  with flowery waves,
And the eagle and cobra on its brow show us
  an inaccessible power.
And the hands clutching a scepter tightly
Never seem to take its hands off to the last,
Therefore from the sunset to the sunrising,
The underground gate of Helios traveling the

사후세계를 여행하는 태양신의 지하관문
그 문으로 황금마차 소리는 사라지지만

파라오의 황금시대는 되살아난다

world after death,

Through which the sound of golden carriage
  faded away,

The Pharaoh's Golden age comes back to life.

중세 도시 겐트*

7세기에 태어나 천삼백 년을 더 살고도
늙지도 병들지도 남루하지도 않은
로마제국 까를 5세가 태어난 영웅의 도시
중세시대 벨기에의 고색으로 덮여 있고
21세기 오늘도 도시 한가운데로 흐르는
레이 강은 곁눈질 않고 세월과 나란히 흐른다
강줄기 따라 양쪽에 지어진 고풍스러운 건물들
한 폭 아름다운 물속 수채화로 되살아나고
종루에 새들처럼 매달려 있는 50여 개의 종들은
짓궂은 바람의 장난에 묘기를 부리기도 한다
종탑 끝 황금독수리상의 예술적 감각에 취한
여행객 발걸음 떠날 줄 모르고
운하를 따라 늘어서 있는 길드 하우스는
그 시대의 권력과 부의 상징을 보여준다
고대와 현대가 함께 공존하고 있는 오늘날엔
보는 이들 시 공간 감각이 즐겁다

*겐트(Ghent) : 벨기에의 옛 도읍지

The Medieval City, Ghent

The city of hero,
In which Karl V of Holy Roman Empire was
    born in 7 century,
Has survived 1300 years more, not being old,
    sick, and shabby,
Is covered with an elegant antique fashions of
    Belgium,
And the river Ray flowing through the middle of the city,
Today, in 21st century flows side by side with
    times without looking aside.
The antique buildings built along the river,
Come back to life as a piece of a beautiful
    aquarelle into the water,
The 50 bells hanging on the belfry like birds
Display their feats the wind's mischief.
The traveler's paces fallen in the artistic sensation
On the golden eagle image cannot be chained
    to its side,
And the guild houses along the canal
Symbolize the power and wealth of that age.
Nowadays, today's travelers have much fun in
    looking at them,
Which the ancient and present ages coexist in.

그랜드 플레이스

벨기에의 심장 미학의 도시 브뤼셀엔
빅토르 유고와 장콕토가 격찬한
'세계에서 가장 아름다운 곳'이 있다
세계문화유산에 등재된 그의 자긍심
지구촌 곳곳에서 많은 사람 발걸음 모여
벨기에 초콜릿과 아이스크림을 즐기는 곳
원형의 가장자리로 둘러친 중세풍 건물은
금실로 수놓듯 화려하게 칠하여져
사람 의상보다 더 예쁘고 멋지게 보인다
관광객들 정신을 빼앗기고
그 장엄한 건물들에 푹 빠진다
지난 밤 가설무대에서 벌어졌던
빛의 향연과 춤 노래 신비스런 음향이
아침의 꽃시장을 위하여 비껴서면
형형색색의 꽃들은 신선한 꽃 내음
앞세우고 걸음걸이도 당당하게 들어온다
오! 우아하고 아름다운 너
꿈꾸고 있나 그랜드 플레이스 광장이여

The Grand Place

There is 'the most beautiful place'
In Brussels, heart of Belgium, the city of aesthetics,
Which the writers, Victor Hugo and Jean
Cocteau praised highly.
Its pride, registered in the Cultural Inheritance of the World
Attracts lots of the people from the global country,
And makes them enjoy its chocolates and ice-creams,
And also makes us enjoyable sight of the
    medieval buildings
Surrounded with an amphitheater, which are
    painted as splendidly as embroidered with
    golden threads,
They look more beautiful and more wonderful
    than our dresses.
The tourists are engrossed in them
And fascinated by the grand buildings.
If last night the light's feast, dancing, songs and the
    mysterious sound
Given at the makeshift stage, stepped aside for the
    flower market of morning,
The various flowers with their fresh aroma at the head,
Appears imposingly before us.
O, you, elegant and beautiful,
Grand Place's square, are you dreaming!

별이 빛나는 창

시계는 중세의 시간에서 멈추어 선 듯 천년의 풍상에
도 고풍스런 멋을 지닌 '해가 지지 않는 나라'의 자존심
을 업고 케임브리지 공부벌레들 하나 둘씩 별을 손에
쥐고 허물 벗듯 연구실 문을 열고 나온다 발목까지 치
렁치렁한 검정 가운 흰색 보타이 등허리까지 내린 빨
간 후드 졸업식장까지 퍼레이드 하며 가는 뒤를 학부
형들 따라 간다 워즈워스의 가슴에 기쁨을 노래하게
한 춤추는 황금수선화 들판을 지나 몇 해 전 펀팅[1] 할
때 노 젓던 아들의 모습 피드백 떠올리며 캠강을 끼고
걸어간다 뉴턴이 식사하던 식당엔 달그락 소리 고요하
고 다윈이 잠자던 기숙사 아직 불 켜지지 않았는데 스
티븐 호킹의 연구실을 눈빛으로 멀리 찾아보며 노벨수
상자들이 꽃처럼 100여 송이나 피어난 연구실들 눈꺼
풀을 이마에 매달고 분초를 깨며 밤을 밝히던 시간은
가고 학위 수여자들의 엄숙한 걸음이 차례로 총장님 앞
으로 나아가 무겁게 무릎 꿇고 앉는다 800여 년 전부터
전통의 맥 이어 온 라틴어

The Starlight Window

As if the time stops in the medieval time, greasy grinds of the Cambridge University with a great pride on their backs of 'the country where the sun doesn't sink.' come out, by one and twos opening their study-room's door as the snake casts off their skin getting a star in their hand. Lots of parents of students follow their graduates parading to the graduation ceremony hall with black drooping gowns to their ankle, the white bow ties, and the red hoods drawn down to their waist. Passing over the field of the golden daffodils that forced to write a beautiful poem to the inner mind of the poet, W. Wordsworth, and coming into my mind a retrospect a few years ago, when my son was punting[1] on the Cam river, I walk along the river. A restaurant in which Newton had dined is silent, and the dormitory's room where Darwin had stayed has not put on the light. I look over not only the room of Dr. Stephen William Hawking far away from here, but also the other ones in which have bloomed Novel

행사 학위증 받는 손이 종이 한 장의 위엄 아래 떨
린다 실낙원의 밀턴과 러셀의 지성의 발자국 소리
아직도 세계인의 귀에 소리 내고 있는 땅 빛나는 전
통의 맥은 오늘도 흐르는 물처럼 한 개의 별만 빛나
던 창엔, 이제 두 개의 별[2] 이 쌍무지개로 뜨고 있
다.

1) 케임브리지의 캠강에서 노를 저으며 배타는 일
2) 아들 며느리 각각의 박사학위 별

바람 속의 하얀 그리움

prize winners like flowers. The time when they have studied competing with one another for their future, passed. Now the graduates kneel down to be conferred a degree one by one before the president. Their hands waver a little under the dignity of a piece of degree written by Latin language, that has been inherited 800 years ago. The brilliant traditional pulse in this land John Milton's Lost Paradise, Bertrand Russel's Lamp of Intelligence have inspired over the whole world, doesn't cease, but is linked like flowing river on. Over the window one star shines, now two stars[2] is suspended by a double rainbow.

---

1) punting: Here it means to pull an oar in a boat on the Cam river.
2) two stars: They mean two Ph.D. of my son and daughter in law.

V.
영혼의 메시지

A Soul's Message

호랑가시나무

골고다 언덕길
예수님의 면류관은
호랑가시나무
겨울에도 잎은
빛을 잃지 않고
초록은 더욱 짙푸르다

억만년이 흘러도
퇴색하지 않을
그 빛이 더하여
가시에 찢긴 이마
핏빛을 토하더니
슬픔의 이슬눈물
붉은 열매 맺은
너 그리스도 나무여

바람 속의 하얀 그리움

A Holly Tree

On the Golgotha's Sloping
The crown of thorns on Jesus Christ's head
Is a holly tree.
It's leaves are deep green
Even in winter
Emitting its light.

Though countless years have passed,
Its fadeless light
Was added to the tree,
And his forehead torn by the Cross
Vomiting blooded color,
You, the tree of Christ!
Bearing red fruits
With its teardrops of his sorrow.

맨살의 길 위에 서서

빈차에 구름만 싣고
휑하니 먼저 떠나버린 차
눈길로 따라 간다
길은 앞 뒤 옆으로
물꼬를 트고 오거리에서
허수아비처럼
두 팔 벌리고 손짓한다

어디선가 상긋한 내음
머리 위에서 내려온다
키 큰 나무 애기사과 꽃
목화송이 같은 순정으로
환하게 웃음 머금고 있다
그 사이로 어머니의
하얀 가르맛길 열려 있는
가고 싶은 길이다

날이 새면 열려진
다정한 이정표가 눈짓하는
수많은 길 있지만
지켜야 할 약속의 길이 앞선다

Standing on the Bare Road

Only loading clouds in the empty car,
The car which has departed quickly
Goes along the road familiar to my own eyes.
The road signals in every direction
Opening an outlet with its hands spread out
Like the scarecrow at a five-way crossing.

From wherever the fresh smell
Falls down over the head.
The smell wears a laugh clearly
Such a pure heart
As the tall trees, small apple blossom, and
the cotton plant.
The white way between them,
I love to go,
Opening like parting mothers' hair.

When it dawns,
There are lots of ways
Where the kind milestone is eyeing,
But the way of promise to keep takes the lead.

말씀 따라 갈 길과 진리
생명 되시는 그 길을 찾아
마음의 눈길을 열어본다

So I open the way of mind's eyes
Searching for the way, the truth, and the life
In His words of the Bible.

나의 하나님

나의 하나님
내 안의 당신은
뜨거운 눈물입니다
내 심장 가장 깊은 곳
베데스타 연못
끓어오를 때
뜨거운 눈물 솟아올라
내 영혼의 강으로 흐릅니다

나의 하나님
내 안의 당신은
새벽이슬에 덮여 있는
뿌연 안개밭입니다
당신을 찾아
밤새도록 헤맬 때
축축이 젖은 발은
내 안식의 강가에 앉아
쉼을 얻습니다

나의 하나님
내안의 당신은

바람 속의 하얀 그리움

My God

My God,
Thou within me
Art hot tear.
When the Bethesda pond
Is bubbling up,
The hot tear of mine bubbles up
Flows as a river of my soul.

My God,
Thou within me
Is a grey fogged bed
Covered with dawn'dews.
When I wander over,
Searching for you through night,
My feet getting wet
Have a rest sitting by the river of repose.

My God,
Thou within me
Is a blossom
Blooming in my heart.

속에서 피어나는
한 송이 꽃입니다
따듯한 바람 사이로
향기를 앞세우고
다가오시는 임
꽃 보다 더 환희로운 모습에
내 눈물은 달달합니다

나의 하나님
내 안의 당신은
가지 많은 포도나무
솟아오르는 붉은 빛의
햇빛살 사이로
걸어오는 금빛 종소리
수많은 가지 중에
내 가지를 찾아 흔들어
종소리 붙여줍니다

My Lover,
Approaching to me,
With thy aroma going ahead,
Between warm winds
More delightful figure than the flower
Bring hot tears to my eyes.

My God,
Thou within me
Is a grape tree with twigs,
And is a golden bell's sound
Walking between the red sunbeams
That are rising up.
It looks for a twig of mine
Among a lot of them,
Shaking mine,
And makes me sound its bell's sound.

울게 하소서

여름성회 기도원
동산엔 햇빛 하얗게 불 내리고
성전 안엔 눈물 비 뜨겁게 내립니다
헐몬의 이슬이 시온 산에 내림같이
안개비 물속같이 차오르니
베데스타 연못이
이곳에 끓어오르니이까

하늘 향해 흔드는 손길
색색의 꽃잎으로 흩날리고
보좌로 가는 길 찾아 헤맵니다
엘리아의 기도에 응답하신 갈멜산상
눈물이 강줄기 되어 흘러내리니
주여! 울게 하소서

'다윗의 고백' 나의 고백되어
'모태로부터의 죄' 원천의 죄를
허물과 연약함 까지도
당신의 사랑으로
온몸 뜨겁게 태웁니다
주여! 그 사랑 위해 울게 하소서

바람 속의 하얀 그리움

Lord, Make Me Cry

At the garden the retreat
For the summer revival meeting
Holy fire descends like white sunbeams,
And tearful rain falls down hotly in the church.
As the dew of Mt. Hermon descended in Mt. Zion,
Filling up like water's inside of fogged rain,
Bethesda pond
Bubbles up here?

Their hands toward the heaven
Ascend up as colorful petals,
Wander over the way for your throne.
The tears on Mount Carmel
Where Elijah's prayer was responded
Flow down as a course of river,
My Lord! Make me cry.

So when 'David's confession' is mine,
Even the faults and weakness of mine,
The original sin, 'the sin from the mother's womb,
Are burnt by your hot love,
Lord! Make me cry for the Love.
Now since two thousand years have passed,

이천 년이 지난 지금도
가시관에서 흐르는 피
그 보혈 한 방울 내 심장에 떨어질 때
주를 위해 울게 하소서
나를 위해 울게 하소서
모두를 위해 울게 하소서

바람 속의 하얀 그리움

When one drop,

His blood flowing from His thorn's crown

Falls down in my heart,

Make me cry for the Lord,

Make me cry for me,

And make me cry for all.

당신의 기적

멀리 뒤로 두고 온
디베랴의 갈릴리 바다는
고요하고 평화롭다
예수님을 따라온 무리들
시장기의 연주 소리가
뱃속에서 꿈틀거린다
가나의 혼인집 항아리
물이 포도주로 변하게 된
예수님의 표적에 아직도
놀란 감동 물보라 친다

보리떡 다섯 개
물고기 두 마리
손에 들고 축사하시니
주의 자비하심 보고
바람도 엎드리고
구름도 발길 멈춘다
잔디에 앉은 사람들
오천 명이 배부르다

무리들 바시시한 머리칼

Thy Miracles

The lake of Galillee in Diberah
Where I left far away
Is silent and peaceful.
The crowds following Jesus Christ
Feel empty in stomach.
They still are moved to be surprised
On the miracle of Jesus that the water is
  changed to wine
At the wedding in Cana.

Taking five barley loaves
And two small fish in his hands,
He gave thanks to God,
The winds hold their breath,
And the clouds stop their steps,
At His authority.
A great crowds, five thousands of people
Sitting on the grass have a full stomach.

Their wild hairs

윤기 내리 흐르고
하늘은 더 높이 푸르고
바람의 행진곡은 신이 난다
열두 바구니 채운
남은 부스러기
많은 사람들이 본 기적이다

바람 속의 하얀 그리움

Are polished nicely,

The sky is higher and bluer,

And a wind's march gets in high spirits.

Twelve baskets filled with the rest
fragments,

Is the miracle that many people experienced.

이새의 줄기에서 한 싹이 나다

저들 밖 산 밑
물소리 낮아지고
양떼들도 깊이 잠든 때
빛난 별 하나
목자를 깨운다
이새의 줄기에서 한 싹이 나
이사야의 예언이
이루어지는 밤
천사가 가지고 온
기쁜 메시지 하나
'지극히 높은 곳에서는
하나님께 영광
땅에서는 기뻐하시는 평화'
구유에 뉘어 있는 아기
경배하러 가는 박사들
메시아의 표적을 본다
세상을 사랑하시는
하나님의 선물
독생자 예수 그리스도

바람 속의 하얀 그리움

A Rod Comes forth from Jesse's Stem

Under the mountain out of the field,
When water sound is low
And a herd of sheep sleep,
One shining star
Awakes the shepherd.
'Coming forth a rod from stem of Jesse',
It's the night
Isaiah's prophecy comes true.
One good message an angel brought,
'Glory to God in the highest,
And on earth peace, goodwill toward men'
The learned men of the Orient
Who traveled to see a Babe lying in the
  manger,
Find the sign of the Messiah.
He is Jesus Christ, the only begotten Son of
  God,
The gift of God,
Who has loved the World.

눈부신 날이 아니어도

눈부신 날이 아니어도
당신을 바라볼 땐
눈이 부십니다

눈부신 날이 아니어도
그림자처럼 언제나
내 곁에 계신 당신
볼 수 있는 영안 열어 주소서

빛으로 몸 감고 오시는
찬란한 그 빛 아름다움
바라볼 수 있는 은총 내려 주소서

시온의 산들에 내린
헐몬산 이슬 밟고 오실 때
이슬 물에 젖은 발 바라보며
내 옷자락 구름처럼 펼쳐서
닦아드리게 하소서

밤이 검은 적막을 둘러치고
어둠이 모든 소리를 삼킨 뒤
당신은 고요히 오십니다

Though It's not a Dazzling Day

Though it's not a dazzling day,
When I look at you
My eyes are blinded by your face.

Though it's not a dazzling day,
Open spiritual eyes of mine
To see you
Who are always like a shadow beside me.

When you come in wearing light,
Grant your grace
Which we can look at its beauty of dazzling light.

When you come stepping on the dew of Mt.
    Hermon
That you gave on Sion's mountains,
Wipe clean it with my cloth stretching like clouds,
Looking your feet soaked in dew-water.

The night encloses with dark loneliness,
After the darkness swallows up all sounds,
You come silently to us.

내 귀는 꽃잎처럼 활짝 피어나고
내 영혼 생명수 물에 씻고 또 씻어
오시는 모습 그리며 바라볼 때
발소리 들리게 하소서

눈부신 날이 아니어도
당신을 바라볼 땐
언제나 눈이 부십니다

I wish to hear the sound of your stepping,
When my ears bloom fully as petals,
And my soul look at your figure
Washing it by the life water repeatedly,

Though it's not a dazzling day,
When I look at you
My eyes are always dazzled by you.

참 포도나무의 가지됨은

이스라엘의 불타는 태양이
여름을 길고 붉게 이끌어 간다
언덕진 곳 기름진 황토밭
타는 햇살이 모여들면
포도나무 그루터기에선
어린 새싹들 몽글몽글
기지개를 펴며 일어선다

밤새 별들과 나눈 밀어는
기름진 흙속에 묻어둔다
신의 아침이슬방울 달고
멀리선 듯 가까운 듯한
사해 바다에서 들려오는
짠 파도소리에 귀 기울인다
감람나무 무화과나무
사이사이를 돌고 돌며
간절한 푸른 꿈 꿀 때

퍼부어대는 태양의
닳아 오른 붉은 숨결
수많은 가지들

To Be the Branch of A True Grapevine

The burning sun of Israel
Leads to the long and hot summer.
If the burning sunbeams
Are concentrated on the sloping place,
Or the fertile yellow field,
The young buds at the stump of the grapevine
Arise stretching itself nicely.

They bury the secret talks
Under the fertile soil,
And listen to the salty sound of waves,
As being far away or near
From the dead sea
With God's morning dewdrops,
And when they dream a blue ardent dream,
Turning round between olive trees and fig trees,

Lots of branches breathing gaspingly
In the pouring sun,
Kiss and stretch one another.

서로 입맞춤하며 기지개를 켠다
하늘을 이고 굳게 버티고 선
나무에 꼭꼭 매달리는 잔가지들
우리도 참 포도나무이신 주님의
가지됨으로 붙어 있어야
좋은 열매 맺을 수 있을 터인즉

As the twigs, hung hard on the tree
Standing up to with the sky on its head,
We have to adhere to the Lord's branch,
The true grapevine tree
In order to bear good fruits.

아무도 모르네

유대를 떠나시다
다시 갈릴리로
우연히 발견한
수가성 우물
잠시 피곤을 풀자
사마리아 여인에게
물 한 그릇 청하셨네
여인은 몰랐네
그가 누구인지
가까이 와 계신 주님
알아보지 못하는 우리
무화과 나뭇잎처럼
말 무성한
헛된 바람 따라
휩쓸려 나갈 때
먼지 무더기처럼
거미줄에 걸리네

차가운 도로에
엎어져 있는
구걸인 볼 때

바람 속의 하얀 그리움

No one Knows

He, leaving from Judea
For Galilee again,
Finds by chance
A well in Suga castle,
And after a moment
Asked a cup of water
To a Samaritan woman.
She doesn't know
Who he was,
So don'we recognize Him,
Who is near by us.
When we live sweeping
Like only leafy fig tree
According to an empty wind,
We are caught by the cobweb
Like a pile of dusts, or the flies.

When we look at a beggar,
Lying on the cold road,
And are in discord

혹시 주님 아니실까
뒤돌아보며 신앙의
자기 시험에 빠져
갈등할 때
우리는 괴로워하네
여인의 거절에
주께서 하신 말씀
'내가 주는 물은
영원히 목마르지 않는
생수가 되리라'
우물가의 여인처럼
헛된 것 구하지 말고
내 샘에 와
생수를 마시라는
주님 음성
날마다 듣기 원하네

바람 속의 하얀 그리움

Doubting he might be a Lord,

Yielded in temptation of our belief,

We feel pains.

Jesus, the Lord says to her refusal,

'The water I give

Shall be a living water

That is not thirsty forever'

And He wants us to hear,

'Don't ask for the vainly things

Like the woman,

Come to the well of mine,

And drink the living water.'

여름 수련장

물안개 걷히듯 장맛비 거두어진
평창 알펜시아 여름 수련장
팔월 산 숲엔 푸르름이 더욱 짙다
투명 날개옷 입은 초록의 향그러움이
신선한 바람타고 안개처럼 퍼져나간다
초목은 훌쩍 하늘 위로 더 올라가고
작은 꽃들은 큰 나무의 옷깃 아래
실눈 뜨고 어여쁜 미소로 하늘거린다
억만 겁 그 이전의 신이 내리신 선물
저 환하게 웃는 빛 부신 아침의 태양이
처음 날의 그 눈부심으로 다가온다

여름 수련대회 열리는 축제의 산 언덕엔
응답의 씨앗 기적의 씨앗 곳곳에 묻혀 있고
말씀은 심령의 옥토를 찾아 육신을 입는다
살아 숨 쉬는 날의 존귀한 시간
온 누리 지으신 신의 권능을 받아 적자

The Summer Training Camp

Surrounding the Summer Alpensia Training Camp,
The forest of the mountain on August is in rich azure
After the heavy rain stops as water-fog clears up.
The green fragrance as it wears on crystal
 wing's dress
Spreads out like fog on the fresh winds.
The grass and tree grows taller up the sky,
Small flowers sway with soft smile
Narrowing their eyes under the branches of
 the big trees.
The nature is a present that God gave us
 countless years ago,
That brilliant morning sun with its shiny face
Is approaching as its splendor of the first
 day of Creation.

On the hill of festival opening the Summer
 Training Program
The seeds of response or miracles are buried everywhere,
And His words wear clothes of flesh searching
for fertile soil.

여린 꽃씨는 여물어가며 세상을 꿈꾼다
태양을 드려 마신 과수의 열매

생명의 빛 내리는 수련장 산언덕엔

응답의 꽃 축복의 꽃

앞 다투어 새싹을 터트린다

During the worthy time of breathing day
Let's write down the moving power of God
 who created all the world.
The young flower's seeds are getting ripe and
 dreaming the world,
And so on the training camp
Which the life's light is falling down
With fruits of an orchard receiving sun,
The flower of response, of miracle, and of bless
Sprout new buds competing one another.

맹숙영 시인 약력

* 성균관대학교 영문학과 졸업
* 한세대학교 대학원 문학석사
* 중, 고 영어교사 역임
* 한국문인협회 홍보위원
* 한국문협 서울지회 이사
* 양천문인협회 부회장
* 한국창조문학가협회 운영이사
* 말씀과 문학 이사
* 한국현대시인협회 이사
* 한국크리스천문학가협회 이사
* 한국창조문학 대상 수상
* 양천문학상 수상
* 시집 : 『사랑이 흐르는 빛』
          『 꿈꾸는 날개』

바람 속의 하얀 그리움

A Brief Record of the Poetess,

Maeng Sook-yeoung

*Graduated from Dept. of English Literature of Sungkyunkwan University, Seoul(B.A. Degree)

*Graduated from the Graduate School of Hansei University(M.A. Degree)

*Taught at Middle & High School as an English Teacher

*A Committee of Public Information in the Korean Writers' Association

*A Director of Seoul Branch in the Korean Writers' Association

*Vice President of Yangchun Writers' Association

*Managing Director of the Changjo Writers' Association

*A Director of the Quarterly Magazine 'Words and Literature'

*A Director of the Contemporary Poets' Association of Korea

*Won a great Prize of the Changjo Literature of Korea

*Won a Prize of the Yangchun Literature

*Poetical Anthologies

"The Light Shining with Love"

"The Dreaming Wings"

역자 / 원응순(元應淳)

* 연세대학교 영문과 졸업(B.A.)
* 연세대학교 대학원 졸업(M.A.)
* 성균관대학교 대학원 영문과 박사과정 졸업(Ph. D.)
* 예일대학교 교환교수
* 경희대학교 영문과 교수, 외국어대학교 학장 역임
* 한국 크리스천문학가협회 회장 역임
* 현재 : 한국크리스천문학(계간 문학지) 편집주간,
          경희대 명예교수, 동숭교회 원로장로
* 영미시 및 소설 번역서, 논문 다수, 그리고 한영대역 시집
          출판(시인들: 김지원, 김지향, 박종구, 최규철, 박진
          환, 유승우, 최진연, 맹숙영 등)다수
* 수상: 한국민족문학 대상(번역문학부문)
          한국크리스천 문학상(번역문학부문)

바람 속의 하얀 그리움

A Brief Record of the Translator

Won Eung-Soon(Ph.D.)

*Graduated from Dept. of English Literature   of Yonsei University(B.A.)

*Graduated from Graduate School of Yonsei University(M.A.)

*Graduated from Graduate School of Sungkyunkwan Univ.(Ph. D.)

*Studied at Yale University as an Exchange Professor

*Taught at English Poetry as a Professor at Kyung Hee Univ.

*Served as a Chairman of the Christian Writer's Association

*Now serving as an Emeritus Professor of Kyung Hee Univ., a Chief Editor of he Christian Writers' Association of Korea, and an Elder of Dongsung   presbyterian Church

*Issued a Few Poetical Anthologies & Lots   of Critical Essays of English Literature

*Translated English and American Poems   and Novels into Korean

*Translated Korean Poems into English: such poets as Kim Ji-Won, Kim Ji-Hyang, Park Jong-Koo, Choi Kyu-Cheol, Park Jin-Hwan, Yoo Seung-Woo, Choi Jin-Yeun, etc.

*Won a great Prize of the Korea Race Literature(for   the Prize of Translation)

*Won a Prize of the Christian Literature of Korea(for the Prize of Translation)

바람 속의 하얀 그리움

2014년 7월 5일 1판 1쇄 인쇄
2014년 7월 10일 1판 1쇄 발행

저   자 맹숙영
번 역 자 원응순
발 행 자 심혁창
디 자 인 홍영민
마 케 팅 정기영

펴낸곳   **한글**
서울특별시 서대문구 신촌로 27길 4호
☎ 02) 363-0301 / FAX 02) 362-8635
E-mail : simsazang@hanmail.net
등록 1980. 2. 20 제312-1980-000009

GOD BLESS YOU

정가 **10,000원**

*

ISBN 97889-7073-398-2-03130